The Coming of the Holy Spirit

Acts 2:1–41 for children

Written by Robert Baden
Illustrated by Reg Sandland

D0324819

CONCORDIA PUBLISHING HOUSE · SAINT LOUIS

When Jesus left the grave alive
    That first great Easter Day
He told the friends that loved Him so
    That soon He'd go away.

"Then *you,* My friends, must tell the world
    My story—all must hear it.
To give you power to do this job,
    I'm sending you God's Spirit."

Then Jesus went back home to heaven,
    And His friends felt sad and lost.
But He sent the Spirit like He said
    On the day called Pentecost.

That morning in the upper room,
Where Jesus' friends went for prayer,
A sudden noise like rushing wind
Roared in as they met there.

And when the sound at last calmed down,
   On every person's head
A burning flame of fire stood,
   Bright and warm and red.

      This was the gift that Jesus sent;
        It gave them power to speak
      Languages like African,
        Arabian, and Greek.

They ran outside to share the news
    With folks from every land.
It made no difference where they lived;
    Each one could understand.

"How can they speak like this?" one said.
   "It's a miracle, I think!"
Most were amazed, but others said,
   "They've had too much to drink!"

Then Peter, chief disciple, stood
   And told the growing crowd,
"The men you see aren't drunk but filled
   With special power from God!

"He's given us the power to speak
   So all can understand
This story that we want to tell
   To those in every land.

"Our Savior, Jesus, Son of God,
    Came down to live on earth.
He came to Bethlehem, and angels
    Sang about His birth.

"When Jesus grew, He told why God
    Had sent Him from above.
He healed the sick, He fed the poor,
    He lived His life in love.

"And then you killed this Son of God;
    You nailed Him to a cross.
You buried Him in a grave of stone,
    Not knowing what you'd lost.

"But three days later He arose—
    Alive, no longer dead!
His death has washed away your sin.
    Come, follow Him instead!"

The people heard what Peter said
    And asked him what to do.
"Turn from your sins and be baptized;
God's calling each of you!"

That day, three thousand people joined
  The church at Peter's call.
And that same Jesus still today
  Is calling to us all.

He's also given each of us
  New power from the Spirit.
Let's share His story everywhere
  So all the world can hear it!

Dear Parents:

You may wish to plan a birthday party with your child as you read this book, for as these events took place, Pentecost became the birthday of the Christian church. Devout Jews from all over the world were gathered in Jerusalem to celebrate Pentecost, a harvest festival held the 50th day after the Sabbath following Passover. Upon hearing Christ's Gospel proclaimed in their own language, 3000 people repented of their sins and were baptized.

The power of His Holy Spirit transformed not only the disciples' tongues, but their entire lives. These formerly timid men boldly proclaimed the saving work of Jesus so all who heard them were stirred by the power of the Gospel.

Jesus has given you and your child the same job that He gave His first disciples, the task of sharing His Good News of salvation with nations (Matthew 28:19–20). The Holy Spirit has worked in you and your child saving faith and gives you the power you need to share God's Word. Celebrate the birthday of the Christian church. Pray that you may boldly share the Good News about Jesus with those around you.

The Editor